Contents

Cracking cliffs

Cliffs are steep walls of rock. They can be hundreds of metres tall. They are found along coasts, in mountains, and even in outer space.

The White Cliffs of Dover, UK

Cliffs are brilliant places to explore.
Are you ready to go cliff climbing?

Creating cliffs

Cliffs are shaped by **erosion**. This is when the wind, waves, and rain wear away the rock. If the rock is hard, it can take a long time to wear away. If it is soft, it can wear away very quickly.

CLIFF FACT
Waves smash into cliffs with huge force, eating the bottom away.

Great heights

Some cliffs are easy for scientists to get to. To reach other cliffs, they need to fly by helicopter or plane.

CLIFF FACT

The world's highest cliff is Great Trango in Pakistan. It is 1,340 metres high. This is about the same as four Eiffel Towers on top of each other!

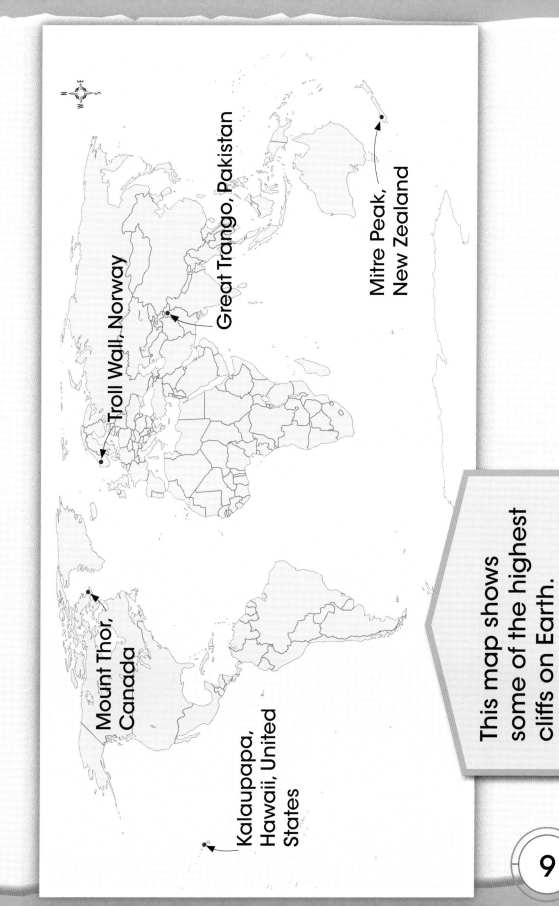

Troll Wall, Norway

Great Trango, Pakistan

Mitre Peak,
New Zealand

Mount Thor,
Canada

Kalaupapa,
Hawaii, United
States

This map shows
some of the highest
cliffs on Earth.

Cliff climbers

Many different scientists study cliffs:
- **Geologists** study rocks.
- **Palaeontologists** study **fossils** in rocks.
- **Biologists** study birds, plants, and animals that live on cliffs.
- **Glaciologists** study ice cliffs.

DANGER AHEAD!
Some people jump off cliffs for fun. This is called "tombstoning" because it is so dangerous. NEVER try this yourself.

Sea cliffs

Some spectacular cliffs are found along coasts where waves wear rocks away. **Geologists** reach the rocks by climbing down the cliff face on a rope. This is called **abseiling**. They have to wear hard hats to protect their heads from rockfalls.

CLIFF FACT
The world's highest sea cliff is Kalaupapa, Hawaii, at 1,010 metres high. That's about the same as ten football pitches laid out end to end!

Kalaupapa, Hawaii, USA

Cliff features

The waves carve out different cliff features. Stacks are cliffs cut off from the mainland. Scientists rock climb up, and **abseil** back down.

Twelve Apostles, Australia

stack

CAVE FACT
Sea caves were once used by **smugglers** to hide their loot in.

Sea caves are holes in the bottom of cliffs. Scientists explore them by diving from boats.

Fossil cliffs

The cliffs along the Jurassic Coast in southern England are 185 million years old. Here, **palaeontologists** have discovered **fossils** of sea creatures, dinosaurs, and sea reptiles.

Jurassic Coast

Fossils like this can be found on the Jurassic Coast today.

pliosaur skull

CLIFF FACT

In 2009 scientists exploring the Jurassic Coast found the fossil skull of a pliosaur (sea reptile). It was almost 2½ metres long! That is nearly as wide as a bus.

Cliff-top colonies

Some cliffs are home to sea birds. Thousands of **gannets** nest on the cliffs of St Kilda off the coast of Scotland. **Biologists** have set up webcams on the cliffs for studying the birds without hurting or disturbing them.

gannet

albatross

CLIFF FACT

About half a million albatrosses **breed** on the cliffs of Steeple Jason, an island near the Falkland Islands.

Mountain cliffs

Some of the tallest cliffs are on high mountains. Scientists can only reach them by climbing. They wear special clothes, boots, and helmets. They are joined together by ropes in case they fall.

CLIFF FACT
Some daring people climb cliffs without ropes. This is called free climbing and is very dangerous.

Ice cliffs

Cliffs are not only made from rock. Huge ice cliffs tower along the coasts of Antarctica and on some mountains. To climb these cliffs, scientists wear special boots with spikes, called crampons, to help them grip the ice.

ice cliff

CLIFF FACT

If an ice cliff climber starts to slip, he or she digs their ice axe into the ice.

Cliffs underwater

There are also cliffs to explore under the sea. They are found in deep-sea valleys, called **trenches**. To study them, scientists have to send down mini submarines, called **submersibles**. They use sound to make maps of the cliff features.

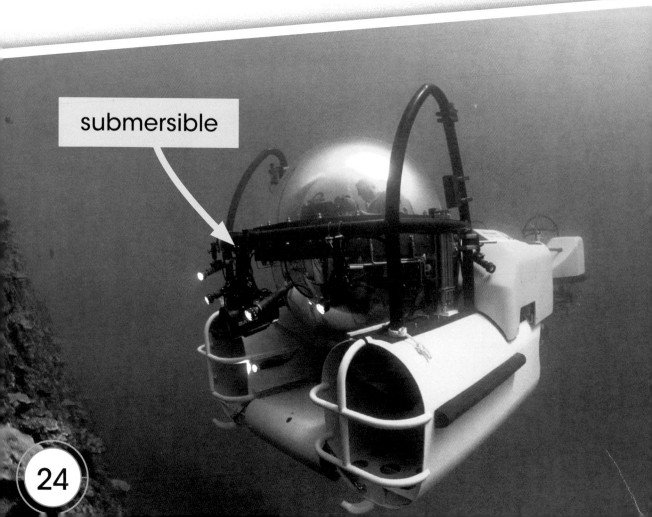

submersible

CLIFF FACT

The deepest undersea cliffs are in the Pacific Ocean. They drop about 8 kilometres. That's about the same as 1,500 giraffes on top of each other.

Crumbling cliffs

All around the world, cliffs are collapsing into the sea. Scientists are trying to find ways to stop this. One way is to use rock armour. This means piling up boulders or chunks of concrete against the base of the cliff.

rock armour

Holderness coast

CLIFF FACT

About two million tonnes of the Holderness coast in northeast England crumbles into the sea each year.

Becoming a cliff climber

If you want to become a cliff climber, you need to be good at science – and have a head for heights! You may need to study a subject such as **geology** at university.

Being a cliff climber is an exciting career. Sometimes, you might be based in a laboratory. You may also get to travel to cliffs all over the world!

Glossary

abseiling way of climbing down a steep cliff on a rope

biologist scientist who studies living things

breed to reproduce or have babies

erosion how rocks are worn away by wind and water

fossil remains of ancient plants or animals that have turned to stone

gannet large sea bird that lives and breeds in big groups

geologist scientist who studies the Earth

geology study of rocks, minerals, and soil

glaciologist scientist who studies ice and glaciers

palaeontologist [say "pale-e-on-tol-o-gist"] scientist who studies fossils

smuggler person who takes things secretly to sell

submersible vehicle like a mini submarine, used for exploring the deep sea

trench deep valley under the sea

Find out more

Find out

What is a fossil?

Books

100 Things You Should Know about Extreme Earth, Belinda Gallagher (Miles Kelly, 2009)

Horrible Geography: Cracking Coasts, Anita Ganeri (Scholastic Children's Books, 2006)

Wild Britain: Sea Cliffs, Louise Spilsbury (Heinemann Library, 2004)

Websites

www.jurassiccoast.com
Hunt for fossils along the Jurassic Coast in Dorset.

www.rspb.org.uk/reserves/guide/b/bemptoncliffs/about.aspx
Bempton Cliffs in Yorkshire is a great place for bird-watching.

www.whitecliffscountryside.org.uk
This site is a guide to the White Cliffs of Dover.

Index